Making Pictographs

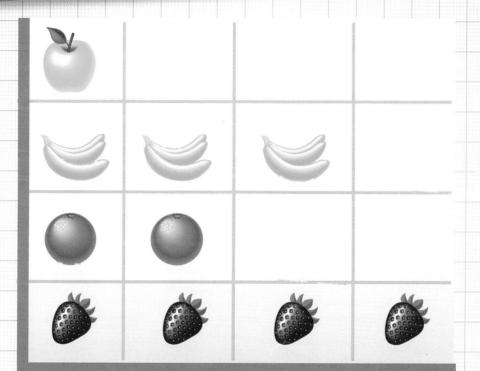

By Kieran Shah

leveled reader
math

Gareth Stevens
PUBLISHING

Please visit our website, www.garethstevens.com. For a free color catalog of all our high-quality books, call toll free 1-800-542-2595 or fax 1-877-542-2596.

Library of Congress Cataloging-in-Publication Data

Shah, Kieran.
Making pictographs / by Kieran Shah.
 p. cm. — (Graph it!)
Includes index.
ISBN 978-1-4824-0843-0 (pbk.)
ISBN 978-1-4824-0842-3 (6-pack)
ISBN 978-1-4824-0839-3 (library binding)
1. Mathematics — Charts, diagrams, etc. — Juvenile literature. 2. Graphic methods — Juvenile literature. 3. Mathematical statistics — Juvenile literature. I. Title.
QA90.S53 2015
001.4—d23

Published in 2015 by
Gareth Stevens Publishing
111 East 14th Street, Suite 349
New York, NY 10003

Designer: Katelyn E. Reynolds
Editor: Therese Shea

Photo credits: Cover, pp. 1–24 (background texture) ctrlaplus/Shutterstock.com; cover, pp. 1, 5, 7, 9, 11, 13, 15, 17, 19, 21 (pictograph elements) Colorlife/Shutterstock.com; pp. 13 (toys), 15 (soccer ball) tele52/Shutterstock.com; p. 19 (photo) Rob Marmion/Shutterstock.com.

Printed in the United States of America

CPSIA compliance information: Batch #CS15GS: For further information contact Gareth Stevens, New York, New York at 1-800-542-2595.

Contents

Boldface words appear in the glossary.

Picture It, Graph It

There are many kinds of graphs. A pictograph is a bit like a bar graph. Bar graphs use rectangles, or bars, to **compare** amounts. Pictographs use pictures or **symbols**. This bar graph and pictograph are showing the same facts.

Books I Have Read

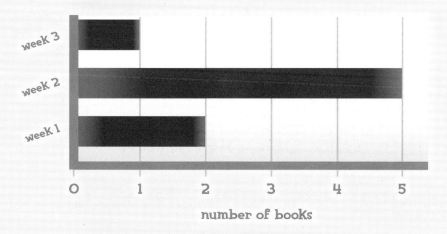

Books I Have Read

 = 1 book

5

The Parts of a Pictograph

All pictographs need a title. A title tells people what the graph is about. Next, a pictograph needs a **key** that tells what each symbol **represents**. This graph's title and key tell us each pencil represents one vote for favorite class.

What's Your Favorite Class?

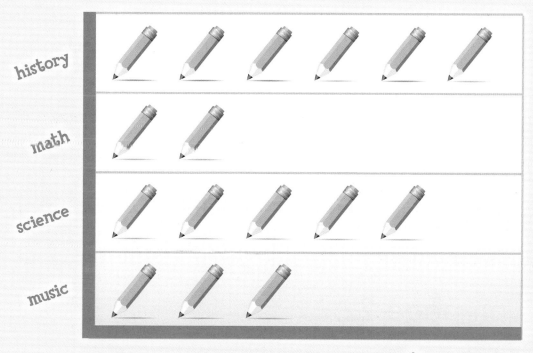

history
math
science
music

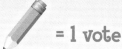 = 1 vote

7

In a pictograph, a symbol may stand for more than one of something. The key will tell you if it does. In this pictograph, how many cones does each picture of an ice cream cone represent? Check your answer on page 22.

Ice Cream Cones Sold

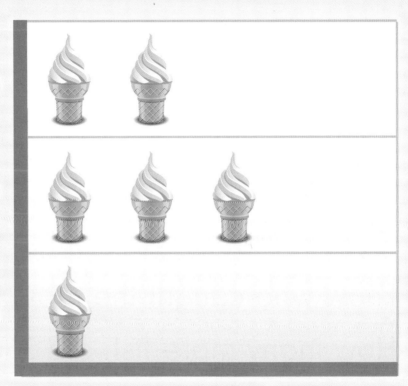

vanilla

chocolate

strawberry

 = 2 cones

9

Pictographs need **labels** for each row. Look at page 11. On the top is a pictograph without labels. On the bottom, the same pictograph has labels. Without labels, you wouldn't know who caught the most fish! How many more fish did Jack catch than Lily?

Who Caught the Most Fish?

= 1 fish

Who Caught the Most Fish?

= 1 fish

Pictograph Practice

A pictograph may use more than one picture. This pictograph is about four kinds of toys in the toy room. It uses a different picture for each kind of toy. How many teddy bears were in the toy room?

How Many Toys in the Toy Room?

dolls

toy trains

games

teddy bears

 = 1 doll  = 1 toy train   = 1 game   = 1 teddy bear

This is a pictograph comparing four soccer players' goals during a season. How many goals does each whole picture of a soccer ball represent? How many goals did Daniel score this season?

Goals This Season

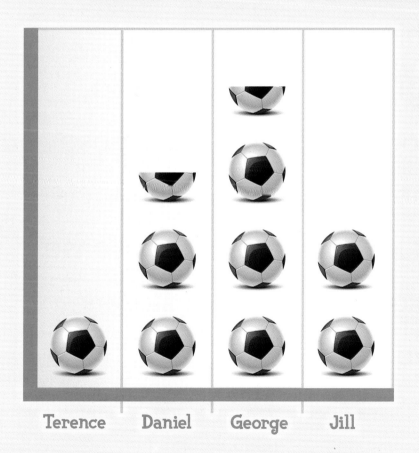

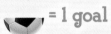 = 1 goal

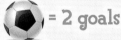 = 2 goals

Terence Daniel George Jill

15

Graphing with Trees

Use this table to make a pictograph. It already has a title you can use. Next, choose a symbol to represent the facts. A picture of a tree makes sense. Let's say each picture stands for two trees.

How Many Trees Were Planted?

Monday	5 trees
Tuesday	4 trees
Wednesday	6 trees
Thursday	8 trees
Friday	3 trees

Now make your graph on a sheet of paper. Write the title. Label each row with the days of the week. Then make a key so people know how to read the pictograph. Your graph should look a bit like this.

How Many Trees Were Planted?

Monday	
Tuesday	
Wednesday	
Thursday	
Friday	

 = 2 trees

Finally, use the table on page 17 to fill in the rows. Don't forget that each picture stands for two trees. How many pictures of trees are in the Thursday row? How many trees does this represent? Now, it's time to make a pictograph about you!

How Many Trees Were Planted?

Monday				
Tuesday				
Wednesday				
Thursday				
Friday				

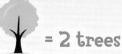 = 2 trees

Glossary

compare: to find what is the same and what is different about two or more things

key: a list that helps explain a graph or map

label: a word or words used to describe something

represent: to stand for

symbol: a picture or shape that stands for something else

Answer Key

p. 8 2 cones

p. 10 1 more fish

p. 12 4 teddy bears

p. 14 2 goals, 5 goals

p. 20 4 pictures of trees, 8 trees

For More Information

Books

Bodach, Vijaya. *Pictographs*. Mankato, MN: Capstone Press, 2008.

Cocca, Lisa Colozza. *Pictographs*. Ann Arbor, MI: Cherry Lake Publishing, 2013.

Edgar, Sherra G. *Pictographs*. Ann Arbor, MI: Cherry Lake Publishing, 2013.

Websites

Pictograph Games
www.softschools.com/math/data_analysis/pictograph/games/
Play games while learning about pictographs.

Pictographs
www.mathsisfun.com/data/pictographs.html
Read about and answer questions about pictographs.

Index